Meerka[ts]

Contents

Written by
Emma Lynch

Northcott School

Meet the meerkats

UK

South Africa

Here is a meerkat.
It is a **mammal** that lives in South Africa.

Let's look at a **mob** of meerkats.

What do meerkats look like?

eye

Meerkats are greyish brown and have black rings around their eyes.

ear

tail

Meerkats have a long body and short legs. They have round ears and a black tip to their tail.

plains

burrow

Meerkats live in **burrows** on dry, sandy **plains**.

Baby meerkats are safe in the burrow.

The meerkats dig tunnels and nests where they can sleep in the burrow.

What do meerkats do?

Meerkats stand in the morning sun to prepare for the day. Then the adult meerkats share the work with their friends.

Some meerkats look out for **predators**.
Some take care of the babies.
They all hunt for food.

Digging for food

Meerkats tear through the sand to find food.

Meerkats hunt for little animals, insects and roots.

Meerkats dig hundreds of holes.
They shut their eyes when they dig to keep the sand out.

Keeping a look-out

The meerkat sniffs the air. It peers around carefully.

Adult meerkats take turns to be look-out. One meerkat stands up outside the burrow and stares around.

If it spots a predator, it barks
'Beware!' to its friends.

Meerkats run back to the burrow if a bird of prey flies by. If a snake comes near, they stand together to scare it away.

When they finish work, the meerkats have a nap in the shade.

Glossary

burrows   holes to live in under the ground

mammal   an animal that has hair and can feed its babies

mob   many meerkats living together

plains   flat land in Africa

predators   animals that kill smaller animals for food